D1567143

This Journal Belongs To:

If found, please call:

_____

Introduction

"Today I'd like to sit and read.
Forget I have a job I need.
Ignore the things I have to do.
And just enjoy a book or two."

Unknown Author

This reading journal was created by an avid reader for book lovers. Its purpose is to help you organize and keep track of the books you've read and the ones on your TBR list.

This journal begins with a table of contents, which also serves as a reading log that you can fill in and use as a quick way to find your notes for any specific book.

The review pages have space to write down your review, thoughts, feelings, notes, quotes, or whatever comes to your mind. There's also a guided rating system, which is a fun way to help you determine the overall rating you give a book.

This journal also includes dedicated pages for your favorite quotes, reading wish list, "top picks," and additional notes.

Moreover, this journal offers the wonderful opportunity to browse through its pages, go back in time whenever you'd like, and relive the magic of your favorite books once again.

From one book lover to another, I wish you shelves full of incredible books and plenty of time to read!

If you enjoy this journal, please support us by leaving a review.

Thank you!

My Reading Log

#	Book Title	Genre	☆
1			
2			
3			
4			
5			
6			
7			
8			
9			
10			
11			
12			
13			
14			
15			
16			
17			
18			
19			
20			

My Reading Log

#	Book Title	Genre	☆
21			
22			
23			
24			
25			
26			
27			
28			
29			
30			
31			
32			
33			
34			
35			
36			
37			
38			
39			
40			

My Reading Log

#	Book Title	Genre	☆
41			
42			
43			
44			
45			
46			
47			
48			
49			
50			
51			
52			
53			
54			
55			
56			
57			
58			
59			
60			

My Reading Log

#	Book Title	Genre	☆
61			
62			
63			
64			
65			
66			
67			
68			
69			
70			
71			
72			
73			
74			
75			
76			
77			
78			
79			
80			

My Reading Log

#	Book Title	Genre	☆
81			
82			
83			
84			
85			
86			
87			
88			
89			
90			
91			
92			
93			
94			
95			
96			
97			
98			
99			
100			

Title:

Author:

Genre: Page Count:

Format   How I Discovered This Book

Bought ◯   Loaned ◯   Gift ◯   (From: _____)

My Review and Notes

_____
_____
_____
_____
_____
_____
_____
_____
_____
_____
_____
_____

Rating					
Plot	1	2	3	4	5
Characters	1	2	3	4	5
Ease of Read	1	2	3	4	5
Quality of Writing	1	2	3	4	5
Overall	☆ ☆ ☆ ☆ ☆				

Date Started

Date Finished

Title:

Author:

Genre: Page Count:

Format   How I Discovered This Book

◯   ◯   ◯

Bought ◯   Loaned ◯   Gift ◯   (From:)

My Review and Notes

_____

_____

_____

_____

_____

_____

_____

_____

_____

_____

_____

Rating					
Plot	1	2	3	4	5
Characters	1	2	3	4	5
Ease of Read	1	2	3	4	5
Quality of Writing	1	2	3	4	5
Overall	☆	☆	☆	☆	☆

Date Started   Date Finished

Title:

Author:

Genre: *Page Count:*

Format	*How I Discovered This Book*

Bought ◯   *Loaned* ◯   *Gift* ◯   *(From:* _____ *)*

My Review and Notes

Rating					
Plot	1	2	3	4	5
Characters	1	2	3	4	5
Ease of Read	1	2	3	4	5
Quality of Writing	1	2	3	4	5
Overall	☆	☆	☆	☆	☆

Date Started

Date Finished

3

Title:

Author:

Genre: *Page Count:*

Format   *How I Discovered This Book*

○   ○   ○

Bought ○   *Loaned* ○   *Gift* ○   *(From:*   *)*

My Review and Notes

Rating					
Plot	1	2	3	4	5
Characters	1	2	3	4	5
Ease of Read	1	2	3	4	5
Quality of Writing	1	2	3	4	5
Overall	☆	☆	☆	☆	☆

Date Started   *Date Finished*

Title:

Author:

Genre: Page Count:

Format	How I Discovered This Book

Bought ◯   Loaned ◯   Gift ◯   (From: _____)

My Review and Notes

Rating						Date Started	Date Finished
Plot	1	2	3	4	5		
Characters	1	2	3	4	5		
Ease of Read	1	2	3	4	5		
Quality of Writing	1	2	3	4	5		
Overall	☆	☆	☆	☆	☆		

Title:

Author:

Genre: Page Count:

| Format | How I Discovered This Book |

Bought ◯   Loaned ◯   Gift ◯   (From:)

My Review and Notes

Rating						Date Started	Date Finished
Plot	1	2	3	4	5		
Characters	1	2	3	4	5		
Ease of Read	1	2	3	4	5		
Quality of Writing	1	2	3	4	5		
Overall	☆	☆	☆	☆	☆		

Title:

Author:

Genre: *Page Count:*

| *Format* | *How I Discovered This Book* |

Bought ◯   *Loaned* ◯   *Gift* ◯   *(From:*   *)*

My Review and Notes

Rating					
Plot	1	2	3	4	5
Characters	1	2	3	4	5
Ease of Read	1	2	3	4	5
Quality of Writing	1	2	3	4	5
Overall	☆ ☆ ☆ ☆ ☆				

Date Started

Date Finished

Title:

Author:

Genre: Page Count:

Format	How I Discovered This Book
📱 ○ 📘 ○ 🎧 ○	

Bought ○   Loaned ○   Gift ○   (From:)

My Review and Notes

_____

_____

_____

_____

_____

_____

_____

_____

_____

_____

Rating						Date Started	Date Finished
Plot	1	2	3	4	5		
Characters	1	2	3	4	5		
Ease of Read	1	2	3	4	5		
Quality of Writing	1	2	3	4	5		
Overall	☆	☆	☆	☆	☆		

Title:

Author:

Genre: Page Count:

Format	How I Discovered This Book

Bought ◯   Loaned ◯   Gift ◯   (From:)

My Review and Notes

Rating						Date Started	Date Finished
Plot	1	2	3	4	5		
Characters	1	2	3	4	5		
Ease of Read	1	2	3	4	5		
Quality of Writing	1	2	3	4	5		
Overall	☆ ☆ ☆ ☆ ☆						

Title:

Author:

Genre: Page Count:

Format	How I Discovered This Book

Bought ◯   Loaned ◯   Gift ◯   (From:)

My Review and Notes

Rating						Date Started	Date Finished
Plot	1	2	3	4	5		
Characters	1	2	3	4	5		
Ease of Read	1	2	3	4	5		
Quality of Writing	1	2	3	4	5		
Overall	☆ ☆ ☆ ☆ ☆						

Title:

Author:

Genre: Page Count:

Format	How I Discovered This Book

Bought ◯   Loaned ◯   Gift ◯   (From:)

My Review and Notes

_____

_____

_____

_____

_____

_____

_____

_____

_____

_____

_____

Rating					
Plot	1	2	3	4	5
Characters	1	2	3	4	5
Ease of Read	1	2	3	4	5
Quality of Writing	1	2	3	4	5
Overall	☆ ☆ ☆ ☆ ☆				

Date Started   Date Finished

Title:

Author:

Genre: *Page Count:*

Format	*How I Discovered This Book*

Bought ◯   Loaned ◯   Gift ◯   *(From:*   *)*

My Review and Notes

Rating					
Plot	1	2	3	4	5
Characters	1	2	3	4	5
Ease of Read	1	2	3	4	5
Quality of Writing	1	2	3	4	5
Overall	☆	☆	☆	☆	☆

Date Started

Date Finished

Title:

Author:

Genre: *Page Count:*

Format	*How I Discovered This Book*

Bought ◯   *Loaned* ◯   *Gift* ◯   *(From:* _____ *)*

My Review and Notes

_____

_____

_____

_____

_____

_____

_____

_____

_____

_____

_____

_____

Rating						*Date Started*	*Date Finished*
Plot	1	2	3	4	5		
Characters	1	2	3	4	5		
Ease of Read	1	2	3	4	5		
Quality of Writing	1	2	3	4	5		
Overall	☆	☆	☆	☆	☆		

Title:

Author:

Genre: Page Count:

Format   ### How I Discovered This Book

Bought ◯   Loaned ◯   Gift ◯   (From:)

My Review and Notes

Rating					
Plot	1	2	3	4	5
Characters	1	2	3	4	5
Ease of Read	1	2	3	4	5
Quality of Writing	1	2	3	4	5
Overall	☆	☆	☆	☆	☆

Date Started   Date Finished

Title:

Author:

Genre: *Page Count:*

Format	*How I Discovered This Book*

Bought ◯   *Loaned* ◯   *Gift* ◯   *(From:* _____ *)*

My Review and Notes

Rating					
Plot	1	2	3	4	5
Characters	1	2	3	4	5
Ease of Read	1	2	3	4	5
Quality of Writing	1	2	3	4	5
Overall	☆	☆	☆	☆	☆

Date Started

Date Finished

Title:

Author:

Genre: Page Count:

Format   How I Discovered This Book

Bought ◯   Loaned ◯   Gift ◯   (From:)

My Review and Notes

Rating					
Plot	1	2	3	4	5
Characters	1	2	3	4	5
Ease of Read	1	2	3	4	5
Quality of Writing	1	2	3	4	5
Overall	☆	☆	☆	☆	☆

Date Started   Date Finished

Title:

Author:

Genre: *Page Count:*

| *Format* | *How I Discovered This Book* |

Bought ◯   *Loaned* ◯   *Gift* ◯   (*From:*   )

My Review and Notes

Rating						*Date Started*	*Date Finished*
Plot	1	2	3	4	5		
Characters	1	2	3	4	5		
Ease of Read	1	2	3	4	5		
Quality of Writing	1	2	3	4	5		
Overall	☆	☆	☆	☆	☆		

Title:

Author:

Genre: Page Count:

Format	How I Discovered This Book

Bought ◯   Loaned ◯   Gift ◯   (From: _____)

My Review and Notes

_____

_____

_____

_____

_____

_____

_____

_____

_____

_____

_____

_____

Rating						Date Started	Date Finished
Plot	1	2	3	4	5		
Characters	1	2	3	4	5		
Ease of Read	1	2	3	4	5		
Quality of Writing	1	2	3	4	5		
Overall	☆ ☆ ☆ ☆ ☆						

Title:

Author:

Genre: Page Count:

Format   How I Discovered This Book

Bought ◯   Loaned ◯   Gift ◯   (From:)

My Review and Notes

Rating					
Plot	1	2	3	4	5
Characters	1	2	3	4	5
Ease of Read	1	2	3	4	5
Quality of Writing	1	2	3	4	5
Overall	☆	☆	☆	☆	☆

Date Started

Date Finished

Title:

Author:

Genre: Page Count:

Format   How I Discovered This Book

Bought ◯   Loaned ◯   Gift ◯   (From:)

My Review and Notes

Rating						Date Started	Date Finished
Plot	1	2	3	4	5		
Characters	1	2	3	4	5		
Ease of Read	1	2	3	4	5		
Quality of Writing	1	2	3	4	5		
Overall	☆	☆	☆	☆	☆		

20

Title:

Author:

Genre: Page Count:

Format   How I Discovered This Book

○   ○   ○

Bought ○   Loaned ○   Gift ○   (From:)

My Review and Notes

Rating						Date Started	Date Finished
Plot	1	2	3	4	5		
Characters	1	2	3	4	5		
Ease of Read	1	2	3	4	5		
Quality of Writing	1	2	3	4	5		
Overall	☆ ☆ ☆ ☆ ☆						

Title:

Author:

Genre: Page Count:

Format	How I Discovered This Book

Bought ⭘   Loaned ⭘   Gift ⭘   (From: _____)

My Review and Notes

_____

_____

_____

_____

_____

_____

_____

_____

_____

_____

_____

Rating						Date Started	Date Finished
Plot	1	2	3	4	5		
Characters	1	2	3	4	5		
Ease of Read	1	2	3	4	5		
Quality of Writing	1	2	3	4	5		
Overall	☆	☆	☆	☆	☆		

Title:

Author:

Genre: Page Count:

Format	How I Discovered This Book

Bought ◯   Loaned ◯   Gift ◯   (From: _____)

My Review and Notes

Rating						Date Started	Date Finished
Plot	1	2	3	4	5		
Characters	1	2	3	4	5		
Ease of Read	1	2	3	4	5		
Quality of Writing	1	2	3	4	5		
Overall	☆ ☆ ☆ ☆ ☆						

Title:

Author:

Genre: Page Count:

Format	How I Discovered This Book

Bought ◯   Loaned ◯   Gift ◯   (From:)

My Review and Notes

Rating						Date Started	Date Finished
Plot	1	2	3	4	5		
Characters	1	2	3	4	5		
Ease of Read	1	2	3	4	5		
Quality of Writing	1	2	3	4	5		
Overall	☆ ☆ ☆ ☆ ☆						

Title:

Author:

Genre: Page Count:

Format   How I Discovered This Book

Bought ◯   Loaned ◯   Gift ◯   (From:)

My Review and Notes

Rating					
Plot	1	2	3	4	5
Characters	1	2	3	4	5
Ease of Read	1	2	3	4	5
Quality of Writing	1	2	3	4	5
Overall	☆	☆	☆	☆	☆

Date Started   Date Finished

Title:

Author:

Genre: Page Count:

| Format | How I Discovered This Book |

Bought ◯   Loaned ◯   Gift ◯   (From:)

My Review and Notes

Rating						Date Started	Date Finished
Plot	1	2	3	4	5		
Characters	1	2	3	4	5		
Ease of Read	1	2	3	4	5		
Quality of Writing	1	2	3	4	5		
Overall	☆ ☆ ☆ ☆ ☆						

Title:

Author:

Genre: Page Count:

Format   How I Discovered This Book

Bought ○   Loaned ○   Gift ○   (From:)

My Review and Notes

Rating					
Plot	1	2	3	4	5
Characters	1	2	3	4	5
Ease of Read	1	2	3	4	5
Quality of Writing	1	2	3	4	5
Overall	☆	☆	☆	☆	☆

Date Started

Date Finished

Title:

Author:

Genre: Page Count:

Format	How I Discovered This Book

Bought ◯   Loaned ◯   Gift ◯   (From:)

My Review and Notes

Rating					
Plot	1	2	3	4	5
Characters	1	2	3	4	5
Ease of Read	1	2	3	4	5
Quality of Writing	1	2	3	4	5
Overall	☆ ☆ ☆ ☆ ☆				

Date Started

Date Finished

Title:

Author:

Genre: Page Count:

Format   How I Discovered This Book

Bought ○   Loaned ○   Gift ○   (From:)

My Review and Notes

Rating					
Plot	1	2	3	4	5
Characters	1	2	3	4	5
Ease of Read	1	2	3	4	5
Quality of Writing	1	2	3	4	5
Overall	☆	☆	☆	☆	☆

Date Started

Date Finished

Title:

Author:

Genre: Page Count:

Format   How I Discovered This Book

Bought ○   Loaned ○   Gift ○   (From:)

My Review and Notes

Rating					
Plot	1	2	3	4	5
Characters	1	2	3	4	5
Ease of Read	1	2	3	4	5
Quality of Writing	1	2	3	4	5
Overall	☆ ☆ ☆ ☆ ☆				

Date Started   Date Finished

Title:

Author:

Genre: Page Count:

Format   How I Discovered This Book

Bought ○   Loaned ○   Gift ○   (From: _____)

My Review and Notes

_____

_____

_____

_____

_____

_____

_____

_____

_____

_____

Rating						Date Started	Date Finished
Plot	1	2	3	4	5		
Characters	1	2	3	4	5		
Ease of Read	1	2	3	4	5		
Quality of Writing	1	2	3	4	5		
Overall	☆ ☆ ☆ ☆ ☆						

Title:

Author:

Genre: Page Count:

Format	How I Discovered This Book

Bought ◯   Loaned ◯   Gift ◯   (From: _____)

My Review and Notes

_____

_____

_____

_____

_____

_____

_____

_____

_____

_____

_____

Rating						Date Started	Date Finished
Plot	1	2	3	4	5		
Characters	1	2	3	4	5		
Ease of Read	1	2	3	4	5		
Quality of Writing	1	2	3	4	5		
Overall	☆ ☆ ☆ ☆ ☆						

Title:

Author:

Genre: Page Count:

Format   How I Discovered This Book

Bought ◯   Loaned ◯   Gift ◯   (From:)

My Review and Notes

Rating						Date Started	Date Finished
Plot	1	2	3	4	5		
Characters	1	2	3	4	5		
Ease of Read	1	2	3	4	5		
Quality of Writing	1	2	3	4	5		
Overall	☆ ☆ ☆ ☆ ☆						

Title:

Author:

Genre: Page Count:

Format   How I Discovered This Book

Bought ○   Loaned ○   Gift ○   (From:)

My Review and Notes

Rating						Date Started	Date Finished
Plot	1	2	3	4	5		
Characters	1	2	3	4	5		
Ease of Read	1	2	3	4	5		
Quality of Writing	1	2	3	4	5		
Overall	☆ ☆ ☆ ☆ ☆						

Title:

Author:

Genre: Page Count:

Format	How I Discovered This Book

Bought ◯   Loaned ◯   Gift ◯   (From:)

My Review and Notes

_____

_____

_____

_____

_____

_____

_____

_____

_____

_____

_____

Rating						Date Started	Date Finished
Plot	1	2	3	4	5		
Characters	1	2	3	4	5		
Ease of Read	1	2	3	4	5		
Quality of Writing	1	2	3	4	5		
Overall	☆ ☆ ☆ ☆ ☆						

Title:

Author:

Genre: Page Count:

Format

How I Discovered This Book

Bought ◯ Loaned ◯ Gift ◯ (From:)

My Review and Notes

Rating					
Plot	1	2	3	4	5
Characters	1	2	3	4	5
Ease of Read	1	2	3	4	5
Quality of Writing	1	2	3	4	5
Overall	☆	☆	☆	☆	☆

Date Started

Date Finished

Title:

Author:

Genre: **Page Count:**

Format   *How I Discovered This Book*

Bought ◯   Loaned ◯   Gift ◯   (From:)

My Review and Notes

Rating					
Plot	1	2	3	4	5
Characters	1	2	3	4	5
Ease of Read	1	2	3	4	5
Quality of Writing	1	2	3	4	5
Overall	☆	☆	☆	☆	☆

Date Started   *Date Finished*

Title:

Author:

Genre: Page Count:

Format	How I Discovered This Book

Bought ◯   Loaned ◯   Gift ◯   (From:)

My Review and Notes

Rating						Date Started	Date Finished
Plot	1	2	3	4	5		
Characters	1	2	3	4	5		
Ease of Read	1	2	3	4	5		
Quality of Writing	1	2	3	4	5		
Overall	☆ ☆ ☆ ☆ ☆						

Title:

Author:

Genre: Page Count:

Format   How I Discovered This Book

Bought ◯   Loaned ◯   Gift ◯   (From:)

My Review and Notes

_____

_____

_____

_____

_____

_____

_____

_____

_____

_____

_____

_____

Rating						Date Started	Date Finished
Plot	1	2	3	4	5		
Characters	1	2	3	4	5		
Ease of Read	1	2	3	4	5		
Quality of Writing	1	2	3	4	5		
Overall	☆	☆	☆	☆	☆		

Title:

Author:

Genre: Page Count:

Format   How I Discovered This Book

Bought ◯   Loaned ◯   Gift ◯   (From:)

My Review and Notes

Rating					
Plot	1	2	3	4	5
Characters	1	2	3	4	5
Ease of Read	1	2	3	4	5
Quality of Writing	1	2	3	4	5
Overall	☆	☆	☆	☆	☆

Date Started   Date Finished

Title:

Author:

Genre: Page Count:

Format   How I Discovered This Book

Bought ◯   Loaned ◯   Gift ◯ (From:)

My Review and Notes

Rating						Date Started	Date Finished
Plot	1	2	3	4	5		
Characters	1	2	3	4	5		
Ease of Read	1	2	3	4	5		
Quality of Writing	1	2	3	4	5		
Overall	☆ ☆ ☆ ☆ ☆						

Title:

Author:

Genre: Page Count:

Format   How I Discovered This Book

Bought ◯   Loaned ◯   Gift ◯   (From:)

My Review and Notes

Rating					
Plot	1	2	3	4	5
Characters	1	2	3	4	5
Ease of Read	1	2	3	4	5
Quality of Writing	1	2	3	4	5
Overall	☆ ☆ ☆ ☆ ☆				

Date Started   Date Finished

Title:

Author:

Genre: Page Count:

Format

How I Discovered This Book

Bought ◯   Loaned ◯   Gift ◯   (From:)

My Review and Notes

_____

_____

_____

_____

_____

_____

_____

_____

_____

_____

_____

_____

Rating					
Plot	1	2	3	4	5
Characters	1	2	3	4	5
Ease of Read	1	2	3	4	5
Quality of Writing	1	2	3	4	5
Overall	☆	☆	☆	☆	☆

Date Started

Date Finished

Title:

Author:

Genre: Page Count:

Format   How I Discovered This Book

Bought ◯   Loaned ◯   Gift ◯   (From:)

My Review and Notes

Rating						Date Started	Date Finished
Plot	1	2	3	4	5		
Characters	1	2	3	4	5		
Ease of Read	1	2	3	4	5		
Quality of Writing	1	2	3	4	5		
Overall	☆ ☆ ☆ ☆ ☆						

Title:

Author:

Genre: Page Count:

Format   How I Discovered This Book

Bought ○   Loaned ○   Gift ○   (From:)

My Review and Notes

Rating					
Plot	1	2	3	4	5
Characters	1	2	3	4	5
Ease of Read	1	2	3	4	5
Quality of Writing	1	2	3	4	5
Overall	☆☆☆☆☆				

Date Started   Date Finished

Title:

Author:

Genre: Page Count:

Format	How I Discovered This Book

Bought ◯   Loaned ◯   Gift ◯   (From:)

My Review and Notes

Rating						Date Started	Date Finished
Plot	1	2	3	4	5		
Characters	1	2	3	4	5		
Ease of Read	1	2	3	4	5		
Quality of Writing	1	2	3	4	5		
Overall	☆	☆	☆	☆	☆		

Title:

Author:

Genre: Page Count:

Format	How I Discovered This Book
▢ ○ ▢ ○ 🎧 ○	

Bought ○   Loaned ○   Gift ○   (From:)

My Review and Notes

_____

_____

_____

_____

_____

_____

_____

_____

_____

_____

_____

Rating						Date Started	Date Finished
Plot	1	2	3	4	5		
Characters	1	2	3	4	5		
Ease of Read	1	2	3	4	5		
Quality of Writing	1	2	3	4	5		
Overall	☆	☆	☆	☆	☆		

Title:

Author:

Genre: *Page Count:*

Format	*How I Discovered This Book*

Bought ◯   *Loaned* ◯   *Gift* ◯   *(From:* _____ *)*

My Review and Notes

_____

_____

_____

_____

_____

_____

_____

_____

_____

_____

_____

_____

Rating						*Date Started*	*Date Finished*
Plot	1	2	3	4	5		
Characters	1	2	3	4	5		
Ease of Read	1	2	3	4	5		
Quality of Writing	1	2	3	4	5		
Overall	☆ ☆ ☆ ☆ ☆						

Title:

Author:

Genre: *Page Count:*

| *Format* | *How I Discovered This Book* |

Bought ◯   *Loaned* ◯   *Gift* ◯   *(From:*   *)*

My Review and Notes

Rating					
Plot	1	2	3	4	5
Characters	1	2	3	4	5
Ease of Read	1	2	3	4	5
Quality of Writing	1	2	3	4	5
Overall	☆	☆	☆	☆	☆

Date Started

Date Finished

Title:

Author:

Genre: Page Count:

Format

How I Discovered This Book

Bought ⭘   Loaned ⭘   Gift ⭘   (From: _____)

My Review and Notes

Rating					
Plot	1	2	3	4	5
Characters	1	2	3	4	5
Ease of Read	1	2	3	4	5
Quality of Writing	1	2	3	4	5
Overall	☆	☆	☆	☆	☆

Date Started

Date Finished

Title:

Author:

Genre: Page Count:

Format | How I Discovered This Book

Bought ◯ Loaned ◯ Gift ◯ (From:)

My Review and Notes

Rating					
Plot	1	2	3	4	5
Characters	1	2	3	4	5
Ease of Read	1	2	3	4	5
Quality of Writing	1	2	3	4	5
Overall	☆	☆	☆	☆	☆

Date Started

Date Finished

Title:

Author:

Genre: Page Count:

Format	How I Discovered This Book

Bought ○   Loaned ○   Gift ○   (From:)

My Review and Notes

Rating						Date Started	Date Finished
Plot	1	2	3	4	5		
Characters	1	2	3	4	5		
Ease of Read	1	2	3	4	5		
Quality of Writing	1	2	3	4	5		
Overall	☆	☆	☆	☆	☆		

Title:

Author:

Genre: Page Count:

Format   How I Discovered This Book

Bought ○   Loaned ○   Gift ○   (From:)

My Review and Notes

Rating   Date Started   Date Finished

Plot   1   2   3   4   5
Characters   1   2   3   4   5
Ease of Read   1   2   3   4   5
Quality of Writing 1   2   3   4   5

Overall   ☆ ☆ ☆ ☆ ☆

Title:

Author:

Genre: Page Count:

Format	How I Discovered This Book

Bought ◯   Loaned ◯   Gift ◯   (From:)

My Review and Notes

Rating						Date Started	Date Finished
Plot	1	2	3	4	5		
Characters	1	2	3	4	5		
Ease of Read	1	2	3	4	5		
Quality of Writing	1	2	3	4	5		
Overall	☆ ☆ ☆ ☆ ☆						

Title:

Author:

Genre: Page Count:

Format	How I Discovered This Book

Bought ◯   Loaned ◯   Gift ◯   (From:)

My Review and Notes

_____

_____

_____

_____

_____

_____

_____

_____

_____

_____

Rating					
Plot	1	2	3	4	5
Characters	1	2	3	4	5
Ease of Read	1	2	3	4	5
Quality of Writing	1	2	3	4	5
Overall	☆ ☆ ☆ ☆ ☆				

Date Started   Date Finished

Title:

Author:

Genre: Page Count:

Format   How I Discovered This Book

○   ○   ○

Bought ○   Loaned ○   Gift ○   (From:)

My Review and Notes

Rating					
Plot	1	2	3	4	5
Characters	1	2	3	4	5
Ease of Read	1	2	3	4	5
Quality of Writing	1	2	3	4	5
Overall	☆	☆	☆	☆	☆

Date Started   Date Finished

Title:

Author:

Genre: Page Count:

Format	How I Discovered This Book
📖 ○ 📕 ○ 🎧 ○	

Bought ○   Loaned ○   Gift ○   (From: _____)

My Review and Notes

_____

_____

_____

_____

_____

_____

_____

_____

_____

_____

_____

Rating						Date Started	Date Finished
Plot	1	2	3	4	5		
Characters	1	2	3	4	5		
Ease of Read	1	2	3	4	5		
Quality of Writing	1	2	3	4	5		
Overall	☆ ☆ ☆ ☆ ☆						

Title:

Author:

Genre: Page Count:

Format   How I Discovered This Book

Bought ◯   Loaned ◯   Gift ◯ (From:)

My Review and Notes

Rating					
Plot	1	2	3	4	5
Characters	1	2	3	4	5
Ease of Read	1	2	3	4	5
Quality of Writing	1	2	3	4	5
Overall	☆	☆	☆	☆	☆

Date Started   Date Finished

Title:

Author:

Genre: Page Count:

Format   How I Discovered This Book

◯   ◯   ◯

Bought ◯   Loaned ◯   Gift ◯   (From:)

My Review and Notes

Rating					
Plot	1	2	3	4	5
Characters	1	2	3	4	5
Ease of Read	1	2	3	4	5
Quality of Writing	1	2	3	4	5
Overall	☆	☆	☆	☆	☆

Date Started

Date Finished

Title:

Author:

Genre: *Page Count:*

Format	How I Discovered This Book

Bought ◯   Loaned ◯   Gift ◯   (From:)

My Review and Notes

Rating					
Plot	1	2	3	4	5
Characters	1	2	3	4	5
Ease of Read	1	2	3	4	5
Quality of Writing	1	2	3	4	5
Overall	☆	☆	☆	☆	☆

Date Started

Date Finished

Title:

Author:

Genre: Page Count:

Format   How I Discovered This Book

○   ○   ○

Bought ○   Loaned ○   Gift ○   (From:)

My Review and Notes

Rating					
Plot	1	2	3	4	5
Characters	1	2	3	4	5
Ease of Read	1	2	3	4	5
Quality of Writing	1	2	3	4	5
Overall	☆	☆	☆	☆	☆

Date Started   Date Finished

Title:

Author:

Genre: Page Count:

Format   How I Discovered This Book

○   ○   ○

Bought ○   Loaned ○   Gift ○   (From:)

My Review and Notes

Rating						Date Started	Date Finished
Plot	1	2	3	4	5		
Characters	1	2	3	4	5		
Ease of Read	1	2	3	4	5		
Quality of Writing	1	2	3	4	5		
Overall	☆ ☆ ☆ ☆ ☆						

Title:

Author:

Genre: Page Count:

Format	How I Discovered This Book

Bought ○   Loaned ○   Gift ○   (From:)

My Review and Notes

_____

_____

_____

_____

_____

_____

_____

_____

_____

_____

_____

_____

Rating						Date Started	Date Finished
Plot	1	2	3	4	5		
Characters	1	2	3	4	5		
Ease of Read	1	2	3	4	5		
Quality of Writing	1	2	3	4	5		
Overall	☆ ☆ ☆ ☆ ☆						

Title:

Author:

Genre: Page Count:

Format	How I Discovered This Book

Bought ◯   Loaned ◯   Gift ◯   (From:)

My Review and Notes

_____

_____

_____

_____

_____

_____

_____

_____

_____

_____

_____

Rating						Date Started	Date Finished
Plot	1	2	3	4	5		
Characters	1	2	3	4	5		
Ease of Read	1	2	3	4	5		
Quality of Writing	1	2	3	4	5		
Overall	☆	☆	☆	☆	☆		

Title:

Author:

Genre: Page Count:

Format

How I Discovered This Book

Bought ◯   Loaned ◯   Gift ◯   (From:)

My Review and Notes

_____

_____

_____

_____

_____

_____

_____

_____

_____

_____

_____

Rating					
Plot	1	2	3	4	5
Characters	1	2	3	4	5
Ease of Read	1	2	3	4	5
Quality of Writing	1	2	3	4	5
Overall	☆	☆	☆	☆	☆

Date Started

Date Finished

Title:

Author:

Genre: Page Count:

Format   How I Discovered This Book

Bought ◯   Loaned ◯   Gift ◯   (From:)

My Review and Notes

Rating						Date Started	Date Finished
Plot	1	2	3	4	5		
Characters	1	2	3	4	5		
Ease of Read	1	2	3	4	5		
Quality of Writing	1	2	3	4	5		
Overall	☆ ☆ ☆ ☆ ☆						

Title:

Author:

Genre: Page Count:

Format   How I Discovered This Book

Bought ◯   Loaned ◯   Gift ◯   (From: _____)

My Review and Notes

_____

_____

_____

_____

_____

_____

_____

_____

_____

_____

Rating					
Plot	1	2	3	4	5
Characters	1	2	3	4	5
Ease of Read	1	2	3	4	5
Quality of Writing	1	2	3	4	5
Overall	☆	☆	☆	☆	☆

Date Started   Date Finished

Title:

Author:

Genre: Page Count:

Format	How I Discovered This Book
〇 〇 〇	

Bought 〇   Loaned 〇   Gift 〇   (From. _____)

My Review and Notes

_____

_____

_____

_____

_____

_____

_____

_____

_____

_____

_____

Date Started   Date Finished

Rating					
Plot	1	2	3	4	5
Characters	1	2	3	4	5
Ease of Read	1	2	3	4	5
Quality of Writing	1	2	3	4	5
Overall	☆	☆	☆	☆	☆

Title:

Author:

Genre: Page Count:

Format	How I Discovered This Book

Bought ◯   Loaned ◯   Gift ◯   (From: _____)

My Review and Notes

_____

_____

_____

_____

_____

_____

_____

_____

_____

_____

_____

Rating							Date Started	Date Finished
Plot	1	2	3	4	5			
Characters	1	2	3	4	5			
Ease of Read	1	2	3	4	5			
Quality of Writing	1	2	3	4	5			
Overall	☆ ☆ ☆ ☆ ☆							

Title:

Author:

Genre: Page Count:

Format How I Discovered This Book

Bought ◯ Loaned ◯ Gift ◯ (From:)

My Review and Notes

Rating						Date Started	Date Finished
Plot	1	2	3	4	5		
Characters	1	2	3	4	5		
Ease of Read	1	2	3	4	5		
Quality of Writing	1	2	3	4	5		
Overall	☆	☆	☆	☆	☆		

Title:

Author:

Genre: *Page Count:*

Format	How I Discovered This Book
⬤ ⬤ 🎧	

Bought ◯   *Loaned* ◯   *Gift* ◯   *(From:* _____ *)*

My Review and Notes

_____

_____

_____

_____

_____

_____

_____

_____

_____

_____

_____

Rating						Date Started	Date Finished
Plot	1	2	3	4	5		
Characters	1	2	3	4	5		
Ease of Read	1	2	3	4	5		
Quality of Writing	1	2	3	4	5		
Overall	☆ ☆ ☆ ☆ ☆						

Title:

Author:

Genre: Page Count:

Format   How I Discovered This Book

Bought ⃝   Loaned ⃝   Gift ⃝   (From:)

My Review and Notes

_____

_____

_____

_____

_____

_____

_____

_____

_____

_____

_____

_____

Rating						Date Started	Date Finished
Plot	1	2	3	4	5		
Characters	1	2	3	4	5		
Ease of Read	1	2	3	4	5		
Quality of Writing	1	2	3	4	5		
Overall	☆	☆	☆	☆	☆		

Title:

Author:

Genre: Page Count:

Format

○ ○ ○

How I Discovered This Book

Bought ○   Loaned ○   Gift ○   (From:)

My Review and Notes

Rating					
Plot	1	2	3	4	5
Characters	1	2	3	4	5
Ease of Read	1	2	3	4	5
Quality of Writing	1	2	3	4	5
Overall	☆ ☆ ☆ ☆ ☆				

Date Started

Date Finished

Title:

Author:

Genre: Page Count:

Format	How I Discovered This Book

Bought ⃝   Loaned ⃝   Gift ⃝   (From:)

My Review and Notes

Rating						Date Started	Date Finished
Plot	1	2	3	4	5		
Characters	1	2	3	4	5		
Ease of Read	1	2	3	4	5		
Quality of Writing	1	2	3	4	5		
Overall	☆ ☆ ☆ ☆ ☆						

Title:

Author:

Genre: Page Count:

Format	How I Discovered This Book

Bought ○   Loaned ○   Gift ○   (From:)

My Review and Notes

Rating						Date Started	Date Finished
Plot	1	2	3	4	5		
Characters	1	2	3	4	5		
Ease of Read	1	2	3	4	5		
Quality of Writing	1	2	3	4	5		
Overall	☆	☆	☆	☆	☆		

Title:

Author:

Genre: Page Count:

Format	How I Discovered This Book

Bought ◯   Loaned ◯   Gift ◯   (From:)

My Review and Notes

Rating					
Plot	1	2	3	4	5
Characters	1	2	3	4	5
Ease of Read	1	2	3	4	5
Quality of Writing	1	2	3	4	5
Overall	☆ ☆ ☆ ☆ ☆				

Date Started

Date Finished

Title:

Author:

Genre: Page Count:

Format   ### How I Discovered This Book

Bought ◯   Loaned ◯   Gift ◯   (From:)

My Review and Notes

Rating					
Plot	1	2	3	4	5
Characters	1	2	3	4	5
Ease of Read	1	2	3	4	5
Quality of Writing	1	2	3	4	5
Overall	☆	☆	☆	☆	☆

Date Started   Date Finished

Title:

Author:

Genre: Page Count:

Format   How I Discovered This Book

⬭ ⬭ ⬭

Bought ⬭   Loaned ⬭   Gift ⬭ (From: _____)

My Review and Notes

_____
_____
_____
_____
_____
_____
_____
_____
_____
_____
_____

Rating						Date Started	Date Finished
Plot	1	2	3	4	5		
Characters	1	2	3	4	5		
Ease of Read	1	2	3	4	5		
Quality of Writing	1	2	3	4	5		
Overall	☆	☆	☆	☆	☆		

Title:

Author:

Genre: Page Count:

Format	How I Discovered This Book

Bought ◯   Loaned ◯   Gift ◯   (From: _____)

My Review and Notes

Rating						Date Started	Date Finished
Plot	1	2	3	4	5		
Characters	1	2	3	4	5		
Ease of Read	1	2	3	4	5		
Quality of Writing	1	2	3	4	5		
Overall	☆ ☆ ☆ ☆ ☆						

Title:

Author:

Genre: Page Count:

Format   How I Discovered This Book

○   ○   ○

Bought ○   Loaned ○   Gift ○   (From:)

My Review and Notes

Rating					
Plot	1	2	3	4	5
Characters	1	2	3	4	5
Ease of Read	1	2	3	4	5
Quality of Writing	1	2	3	4	5
Overall	☆	☆	☆	☆	☆

Date Started   Date Finished

Title:

Author:

Genre: Page Count:

Format	How I Discovered This Book

Bought ○   Loaned ○   Gift ○   (From:)

My Review and Notes

Rating					
Plot	1	2	3	4	5
Characters	1	2	3	4	5
Ease of Read	1	2	3	4	5
Quality of Writing	1	2	3	4	5
Overall	☆ ☆ ☆ ☆ ☆				

Date Started

Date Finished

Title:

Author:

Genre: Page Count:

Format   How I Discovered This Book

Bought ◯   Loaned ◯   Gift ◯   (From:)

My Review and Notes

Rating						Date Started	Date Finished
Plot	1	2	3	4	5		
Characters	1	2	3	4	5		
Ease of Read	1	2	3	4	5		
Quality of Writing	1	2	3	4	5		
Overall	☆	☆	☆	☆	☆		

Title:

Author:

Genre: Page Count:

Format   How I Discovered This Book

○   ○   ○

Bought ○   Loaned ○   Gift ○   (From:)

My Review and Notes

Rating					
Plot	1	2	3	4	5
Characters	1	2	3	4	5
Ease of Read	1	2	3	4	5
Quality of Writing	1	2	3	4	5
Overall	☆	☆	☆	☆	☆

Date Started

Date Finished

Title:

Author:

Genre: Page Count:

Format   How I Discovered This Book

Bought ◯   Loaned ◯   Gift ◯   (From:)

My Review and Notes

Rating		Date Started	Date Finished

Rating

Plot   1 2 3 4 5
Characters   1 2 3 4 5
Ease of Read   1 2 3 4 5
Quality of Writing 1 2 3 4 5

Overall   ☆☆☆☆☆

Title:

Author:

Genre: Page Count:

Format	How I Discovered This Book

Bought ⚪   Loaned ⚪   Gift ⚪   (From: _____)

My Review and Notes

_____

_____

_____

_____

_____

_____

_____

_____

_____

_____

_____

_____

Rating						Date Started	Date Finished
Plot	1	2	3	4	5		
Characters	1	2	3	4	5		
Ease of Read	1	2	3	4	5		
Quality of Writing	1	2	3	4	5		
Overall	☆	☆	☆	☆	☆		

Title:

Author:

Genre: Page Count:

Format   How I Discovered This Book

Bought ◯   Loaned ◯   Gift ◯   (From:)

My Review and Notes

Rating						Date Started	Date Finished
Plot	1	2	3	4	5		
Characters	1	2	3	4	5		
Ease of Read	1	2	3	4	5		
Quality of Writing	1	2	3	4	5		
Overall	☆ ☆ ☆ ☆ ☆						

Title:

Author:

Genre: Page Count:

| Format | How I Discovered This Book |

Bought ○   Loaned ○   Gift ○   (From:)

My Review and Notes

Rating					
Plot	1	2	3	4	5
Characters	1	2	3	4	5
Ease of Read	1	2	3	4	5
Quality of Writing	1	2	3	4	5
Overall	☆ ☆ ☆ ☆ ☆				

Date Started   Date Finished

Title:

Author:

Genre: Page Count:

Format   How I Discovered This Book

Bought ○   Loaned ○   Gift ○   (From:)

My Review and Notes

Rating					
Plot	1	2	3	4	5
Characters	1	2	3	4	5
Ease of Read	1	2	3	4	5
Quality of Writing	1	2	3	4	5
Overall	☆	☆	☆	☆	☆

Date Started

Date Finished

Title:

Author:

Genre: Page Count:

Format	How I Discovered This Book

Bought ○   Loaned ○   Gift ○   (From:)

My Review and Notes

Rating						Date Started	Date Finished
Plot	1	2	3	4	5		
Characters	1	2	3	4	5		
Ease of Read	1	2	3	4	5		
Quality of Writing	1	2	3	4	5		
Overall	☆	☆	☆	☆	☆		

Title:

Author:

Genre: Page Count:

Format   How I Discovered This Book

○   ○   ○

Bought ○   Loaned ○   Gift ○   (From:)

My Review and Notes

Rating					
Plot	1	2	3	4	5
Characters	1	2	3	4	5
Ease of Read	1	2	3	4	5
Quality of Writing	1	2	3	4	5
Overall	☆ ☆ ☆ ☆ ☆				

Date Started   Date Finished

Title:

Author:

Genre: Page Count:

Format   How I Discovered This Book

Bought ○   Loaned ○   Gift ○   (From:)

My Review and Notes

Rating					
Plot	1	2	3	4	5
Characters	1	2	3	4	5
Ease of Read	1	2	3	4	5
Quality of Writing	1	2	3	4	5
Overall	☆	☆	☆	☆	☆

Date Started   Date Finished

Title:

Author:

Genre: *Page Count:*

Format   *How I Discovered This Book*

Bought ◯   *Loaned* ◯   *Gift* ◯   *(From:*   *)*

My Review and Notes

Rating					
Plot	1	2	3	4	5
Characters	1	2	3	4	5
Ease of Read	1	2	3	4	5
Quality of Writing	1	2	3	4	5
Overall	☆	☆	☆	☆	☆

Date Started   *Date Finished*

Title:

Author:

Genre: Page Count:

Format   How I Discovered This Book

Bought ◯   Loaned ◯   Gift ◯ (From:)

My Review and Notes

Rating				
Plot	1	2	3	4	5
Characters	1	2	3	4	5
Ease of Read	1	2	3	4	5
Quality of Writing	1	2	3	4	5
Overall	☆☆☆☆☆				

Date Started   Date Finished

Title:

Author:

Genre: Page Count:

Format   How I Discovered This Book

Bought ◯   Loaned ◯   Gift ◯   (From:)

My Review and Notes

Rating					
Plot	1	2	3	4	5
Characters	1	2	3	4	5
Ease of Read	1	2	3	4	5
Quality of Writing	1	2	3	4	5
Overall	☆	☆	☆	☆	☆

Date Started   Date Finished

Title:

Author:

Genre: *Page Count:*

Format	How I Discovered This Book
📱 ◯ 📖 ◯ 🎧 ◯	

Bought ◯   *Loaned* ◯   *Gift* ◯   *(From:* _____ *)*

My Review and Notes

_____

_____

_____

_____

_____

_____

_____

_____

_____

_____

_____

Rating					
Plot	1	2	3	4	5
Characters	1	2	3	4	5
Ease of Read	1	2	3	4	5
Quality of Writing	1	2	3	4	5
Overall	☆	☆	☆	☆	☆

Date Started   *Date Finished*

Title:

Author:

Genre: _____ *Page Count:* _____

| Format | How I Discovered This Book |

Bought ◯   *Loaned* ◯   *Gift* ◯   *(From:* _____ *)*

My Review and Notes

_____
_____
_____
_____
_____
_____
_____
_____
_____
_____
_____
_____

Rating					
Plot	1	2	3	4	5
Characters	1	2	3	4	5
Ease of Read	1	2	3	4	5
Quality of Writing	1	2	3	4	5
Overall	☆	☆	☆	☆	☆

Date Started _____   *Date Finished* _____

Title:

Author:

Genre: Page Count:

Format	How I Discovered This Book

Bought ◯   Loaned ◯   Gift ◯   (From:)

My Review and Notes

_____

_____

_____

_____

_____

_____

_____

_____

_____

_____

_____

_____

Rating					
Plot	1	2	3	4	5
Characters	1	2	3	4	5
Ease of Read	1	2	3	4	5
Quality of Writing	1	2	3	4	5
Overall	☆	☆	☆	☆	☆

Date Started

Date Finished

Title:

Author:

Genre: Page Count:

Format	How I Discovered This Book

Bought ◯   Loaned ◯   Gift ◯   (From:)

My Review and Notes

Rating					
Plot	1	2	3	4	5
Characters	1	2	3	4	5
Ease of Read	1	2	3	4	5
Quality of Writing	1	2	3	4	5
Overall	☆☆☆☆☆				

Date Started

Date Finished

Title:

Author:

Genre: *Page Count:*

Format	How I Discovered This Book

Bought ◯   Loaned ◯   Gift ◯   (From: _____)

My Review and Notes

Rating					
Plot	1	2	3	4	5
Characters	1	2	3	4	5
Ease of Read	1	2	3	4	5
Quality of Writing	1	2	3	4	5
Overall	☆ ☆ ☆ ☆ ☆				

Date Started   *Date Finished*

Title:

Author:

Genre: Page Count:

Format	How I Discovered This Book

Bought ⃝   Loaned ⃝   Gift ⃝ (From: _____)

My Review and Notes

_____

_____

_____

_____

_____

_____

_____

_____

_____

_____

_____

Rating						Date Started	Date Finished
Plot	1	2	3	4	5		
Characters	1	2	3	4	5		
Ease of Read	1	2	3	4	5		
Quality of Writing	1	2	3	4	5		
Overall	☆	☆	☆	☆	☆		

Top Picks

Favorite Quotes

Favorite Quotes

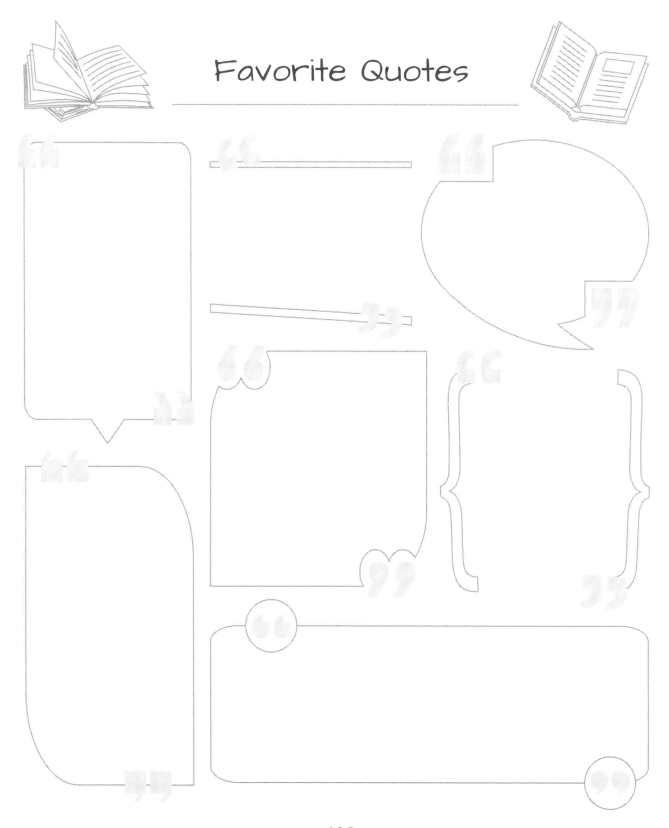

Reading Wish List

☐ - Book title   ✒ - Author   👍 - Recommended by

☐	☐	☐	☐
✒	✒	✒	✒
👍	👍	👍	👍
Read ○	Read ○	Read ○	Read ○
☐	☐	☐	☐
✒	✒	✒	✒
👍	👍	👍	👍
Read ○	Read ○	Read ○	Read ○
☐	☐	☐	☐
✒	✒	✒	✒
👍	👍	👍	👍
Read ○	Read ○	Read ○	Read ○
☐	☐	☐	☐
✒	✒	✒	✒
👍	👍	👍	👍
Read ○	Read ○	Read ○	Read ○

Reading Wish List

☐ - Book title   ✒ - Author   👍⭐ - Recommended by

☐	☐	☐	☐
✒	✒	✒	✒
👍⭐	👍⭐	👍⭐	👍⭐
Read ○	Read ○	Read ○	Read ○
☐	☐	☐	☐
✒	✒	✒	✒
👍⭐	👍⭐	👍⭐	👍⭐
Read ○	Read ○	Read ○	Read ○
☐	☐	☐	☐
✒	✒	✒	✒
👍⭐	👍⭐	👍⭐	👍⭐
Read ○	Read ○	Read ○	Read ○
☐	☐	☐	☐
✒	✒	✒	✒
👍⭐	👍⭐	👍⭐	👍⭐
Read ○	Read ○	Read ○	Read ○

Reading Wish List

- Book title   - Author   - Recommended by

Read ○   Read ○   Read ○   Read ○

Read ○   Read ○   Read ○   Read ○

Read ○   Read ○   Read ○   Read ○

Read ○   Read ○   Read ○   Read ○

Reading Wish List

☐ - *Book title* ✒ - *Author* 👍⭐ - *Recommended by*

☐	☐	☐	☐
✒	✒	✒	✒
👍⭐	👍⭐	👍⭐	👍⭐
Read ○	*Read* ○	*Read* ○	*Read* ○
☐	☐	☐	☐
✒	✒	✒	✒
👍⭐	👍⭐	👍⭐	👍⭐
Read ○	*Read* ○	*Read* ○	*Read* ○
☐	☐	☐	☐
✒	✒	✒	✒
👍⭐	👍⭐	👍⭐	👍⭐
Read ○	*Read* ○	*Read* ○	*Read* ○
☐	☐	☐	☐
✒	✒	✒	✒
👍⭐	👍⭐	👍⭐	👍⭐
Read ○	*Read* ○	*Read* ○	*Read* ○

Notes

Notes